TABLE OF CONTENTS
DISCLAIMER AND TERMS OF USE AGREEMENT:

Create A List

Web Form

Body

Labels

Inputs

Submit

Confirmed Opt-In

Follow Up Messages

I Have a Special Gift for My Readers

Meet the Author

AWeber Primer
Email Marketing the Legal Way!
©Copyright 2013 by Leland Benton

DISCLAIMER AND TERMS OF USE AGREEMENT:

(Please Read This Before Using This Book)
This information is for educational and informational purposes only. The content is not intended to be a substitute for any professional advice, diagnosis, or treatment.

The authors and publisher of this book and the accompanying materials have used their best efforts in preparing this book.

The authors and publisher make no representation or warranties with respect to the accuracy, applicability, fitness, or completeness of the contents of this book. The information contained in this book is strictly for educational purposes. Therefore, if you wish to apply ideas contained in this book, you are taking full responsibility for your actions.

The authors and publisher disclaim any warranties (express or implied), merchantability, or fitness for any particular purpose. The author and publisher shall in no event be held liable to any party for any direct, indirect, punitive, special, incidental or other consequential damages arising directly or indirectly from any use of this material, which is provided "as is", and without warranties. As always, the advice of a competent legal, tax, accounting, medical or other professional should be sought where applicable.

The authors and publisher do not warrant the performance, effectiveness or applicability of any sites listed or linked to in this book. All links are for information purposes only and are not warranted for content, accuracy or any other implied or explicit purpose. No part of this may be copied, or changed in any format, or used in any way other than what is outlined within this course under any circumstances. Violators will be prosecuted.

This book is © Copyrighted by ePubWealth.com.

Get AWeber now at a special introductory rate of $1 for the first month and then $19/ month. Go here:
http://bit.ly/NMxDo

Create A List

Log into AWeber this is the first screen you will see.

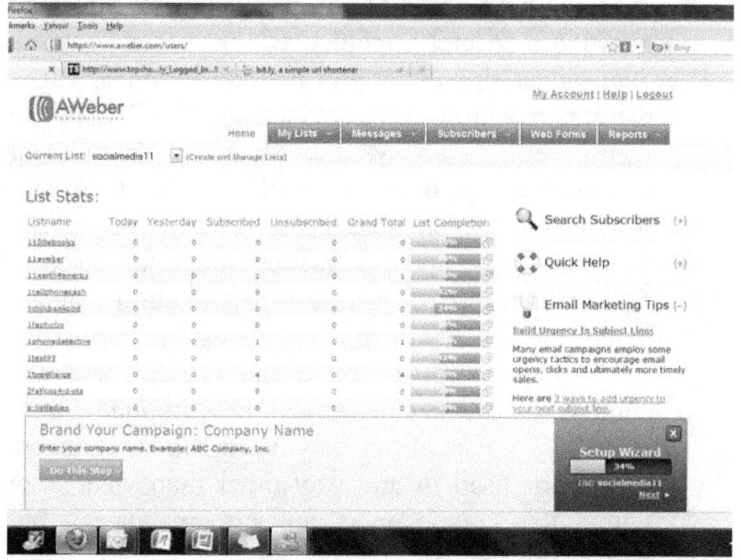

As you see most of my lists are only at about 50% done.

You do not need to have them at 100% at this point in time.

Just finish it as much as you need it to be finished for now and we will go back and finish it later.

The most important thing right now is to get a list started and an opt-in box made.

After that is done we will go back and finish out the rest.

Click on (Create and Manage) Lists at the top and you will be taken to the following page.

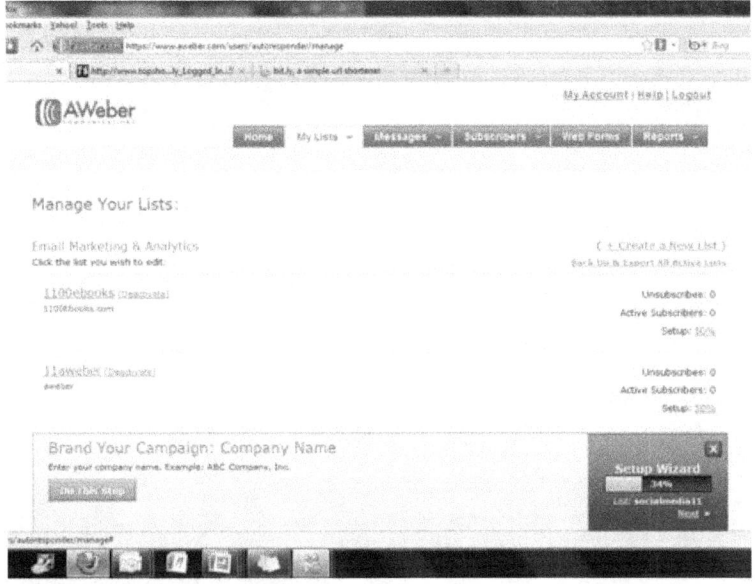

Notice again that my lists are only 50% finished at this point in time. Here you click on (+ Create a New List)

List Settings: You will see this…

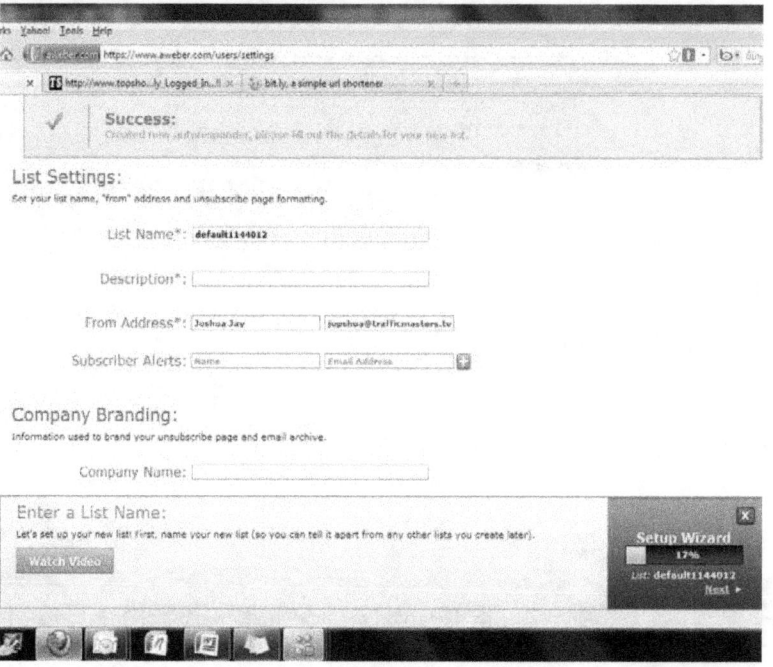

Now fill in the List name.

This has to be a unique name to all of AWeber so you may need to be creative and put some numbers or something after it.

Fill in the description.

This can be anything that you want.

It will show up on the page of lists under the list name so you know what the list is.

The From Address will already be filled in.

Subscriber alerts – this is the email that you want AWeber to notify you at when someone fills out your Webform so you know that someone is on your list.

So put your email here.

Press the green +.

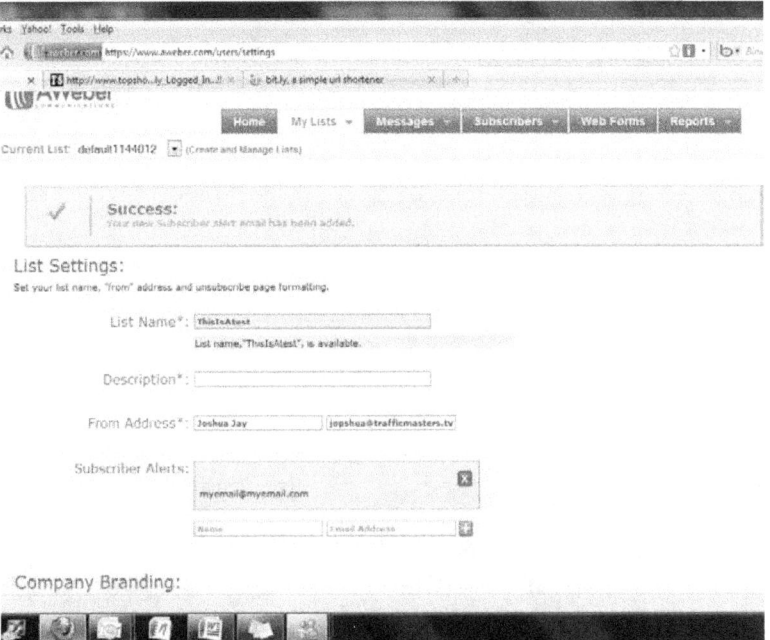

I leave the name blank lots of time.

As far as the rest of this page there is no need to fill it out right now.

The company branding is information that your subscriber will see on "the unsubscribe" and confirmation links.

I usually leave this blank right now and come back to it later after I get the Webform finished.

However for this example we will fill it in now.

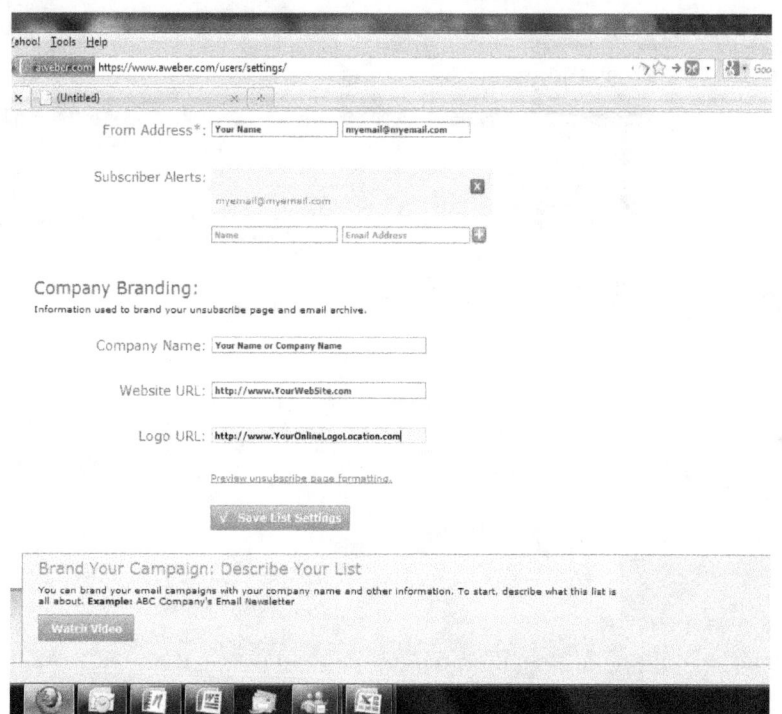

Company Name – this is the name that you want the signature to be in the confirmation email that your website visitor will receive when they fill in their name and email in your opt-in box.

Website – This is your website

Logo URL – this is the URL where your logo is located on the internet

Click on "Save List Settings" – if you have it all right then it will tell you it saved successfully. It will look like this.

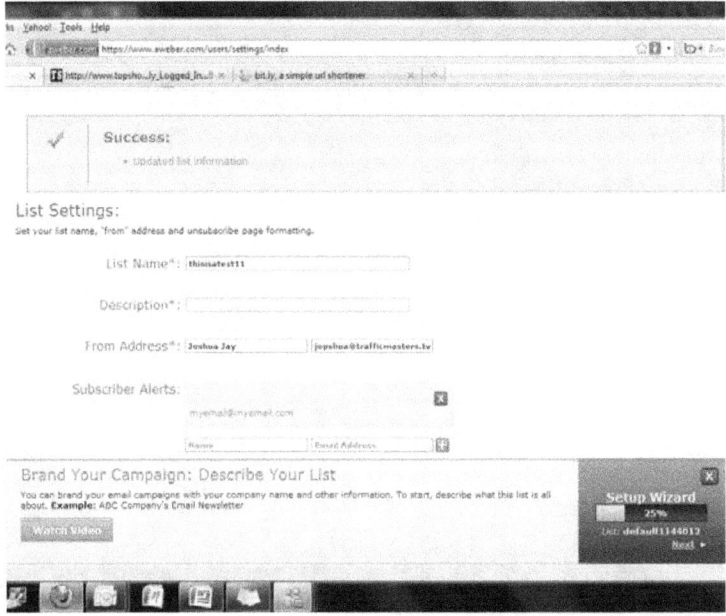

As you can see I had to go back and change my list name because even though it told me at first that the name was available when I tried to save it, it came back and told me that the list name was taken so I had to amend it and save again.

Now you are done on this page. Go to the top of the page and make sure that the list you just created is in the box that says current list and then click on Web Forms.

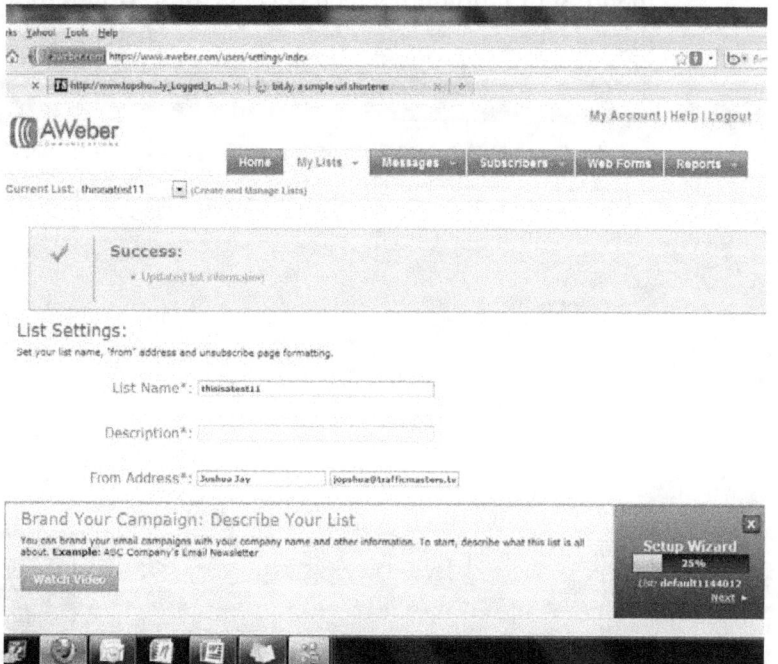

Here you see that the current list is "thisisatest11" which is the list I just created.

To get back to this list later to make changes just click on the drop down arrow and all of your lists will show.

Choose the list you want.

Web Form

Now we are going to click on the Blue Web Forms tab and you will see this.

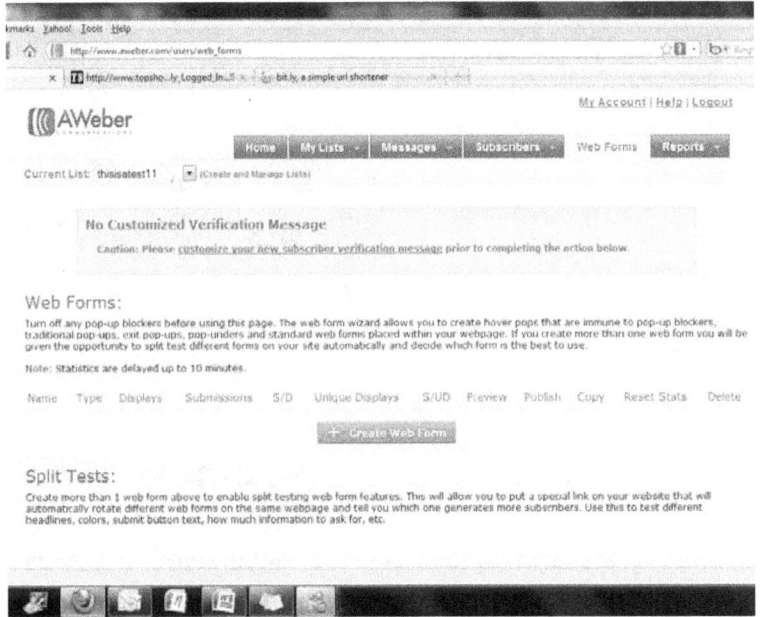

We do not have any web forms for this list yet so click on create web form in the green box.

If there were already web forms made they would be listed and you could click on them to edit them.

Click on the green box that says "+Create Web Form"

Now you are here…

You can use one of AWeber's templates or you can make your own.

I will show you how to make your own because then you will be able to change AWeber's templates as you want them also.

If you have already made some templates you can also click on My Templates and choose one that you have already made.

For this example I will just start from scratch and make a new template.

So the first thing I do is click on the arrow beside hide templates so that is out of my way then I will put in my width.

This is the form I have been using for the pop-overs I have made.

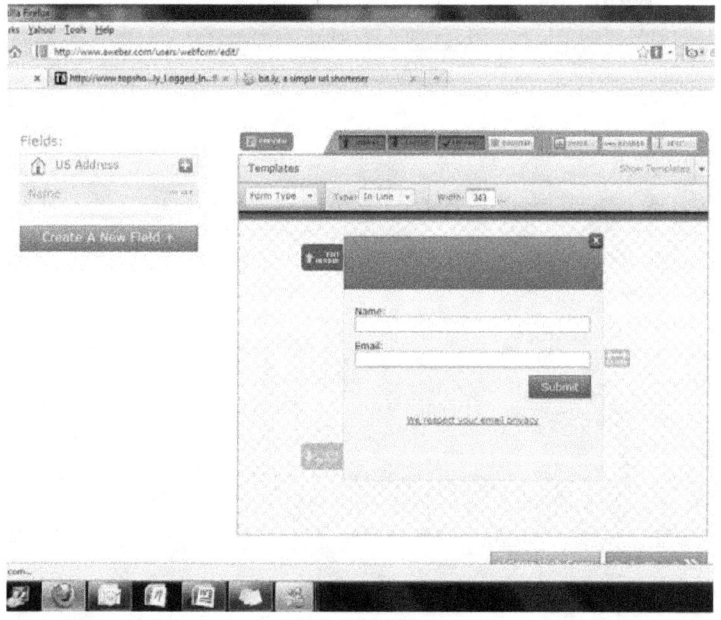

Now you see there is a red box with an x in it. I will click on that to get rid of the Header.

If I move my pointer down the left hand side of the box I will find more red boxes and I will get rid of everything except for the body.

You can leave or get rid of any of these as you want.

This is just how I have been doing this box.

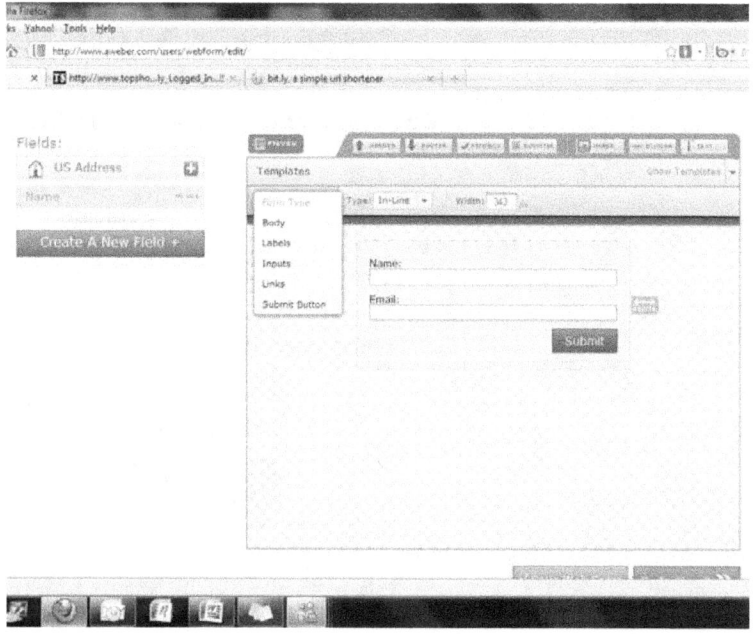

It will look like this.

From here I click on the down arrow next to form type and choose body.

I will go through each of these and set the settings that I want. I am just going to show what it looks like on each one when I am finsihed with the settings.

Body

I put "000000" in for the background color to make it black.

Click on the color square to the right of backgrounds to do this.

Another window opens that lets you change the color.

Labels

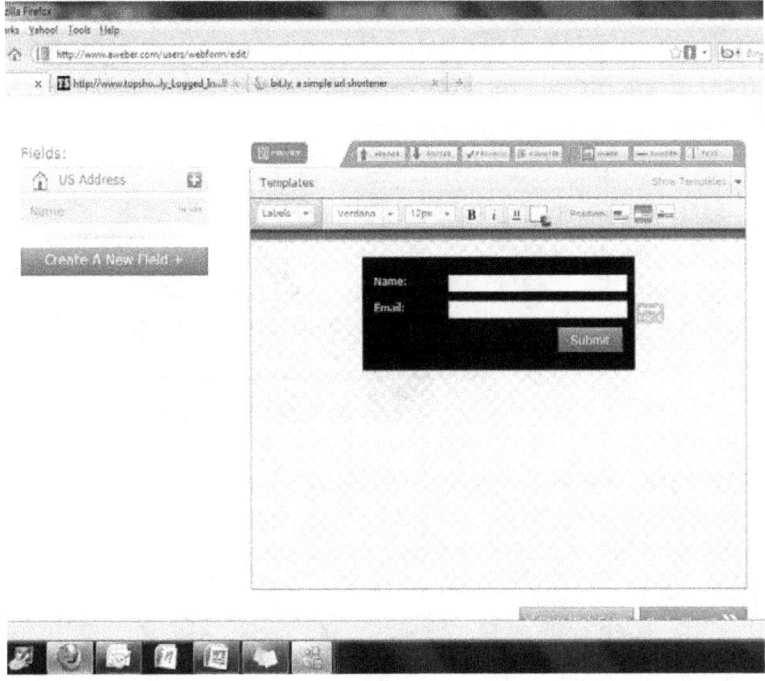

I choose the position of the labels on this by clicking on the middle icon to the left of positions.

Inputs

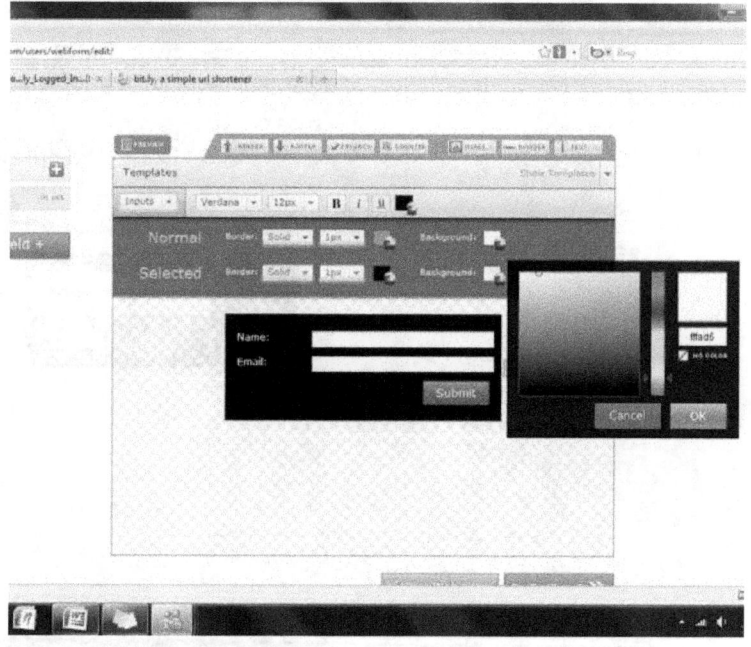

Here I clicked on the down arrows by advanced.

This is covered up by the color box right now.

You need to change the color to white here or you will have problems later.

Do this by putting "ffffff" in the box where you see "fffad6" right now and click ok.

Submit

I want my submit box to be white so I click on the blue box next to colors and change the code to "ffffff", I also want my box in the middle so I choose that, it is behind the color box right now next to the blue box. It gives you a choice of left, center or right. Now I am going to enter my wording. I have this in a word doc so I can just copy and paste then make changes as needed. I will click on the text button in the top right hand corner and a text box will pop up

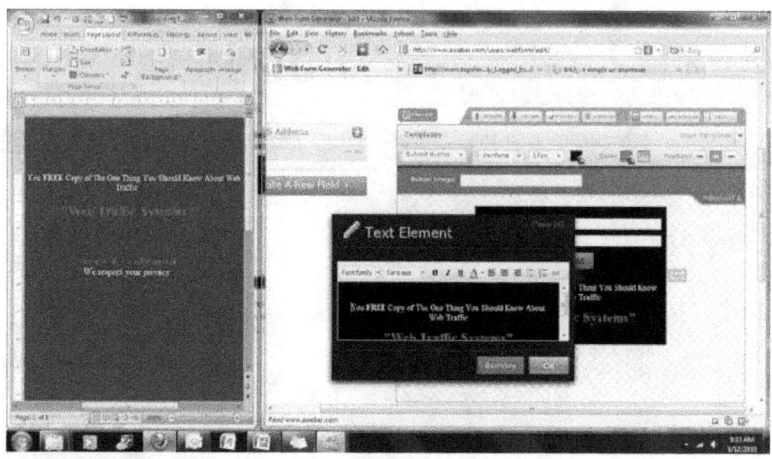

I click on ok

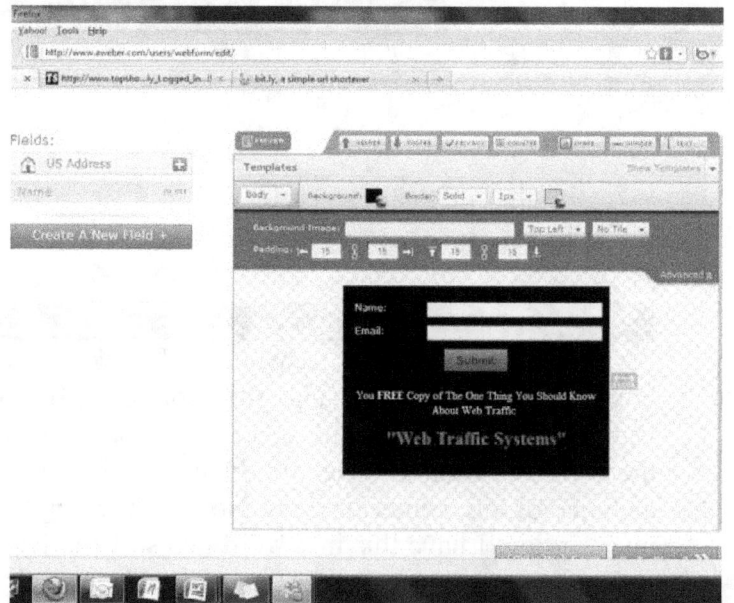

Now I put my pointer on top of the wording and hold down the right mouse button and move it to the top I can also click on the edit button by doing this to edit the text

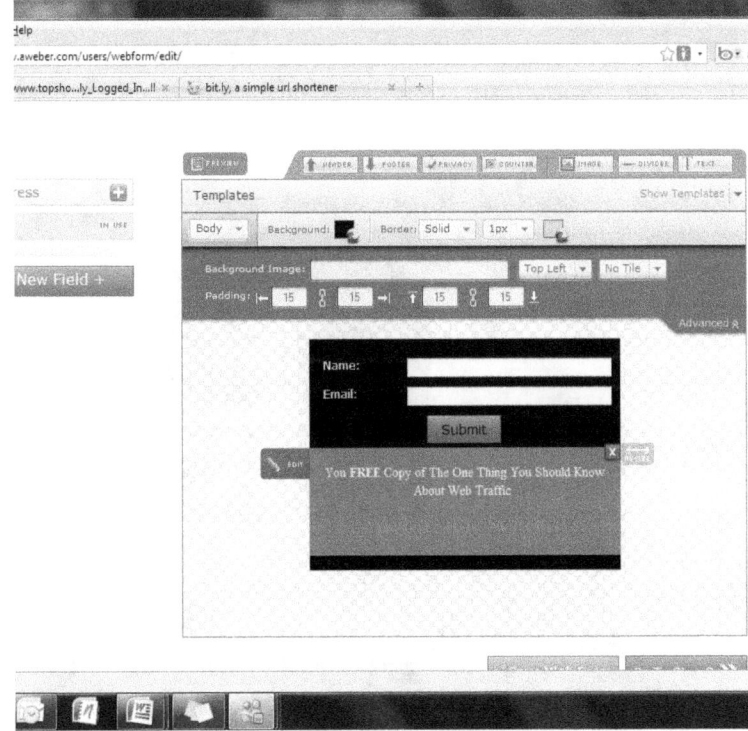

I repeat this to put in my disclaimer I will also fix my submit button as I forgot to click ok to make it white so it will be white in the next picture

Now, to insert the picture: I click on image to the left of text on the top bar and a window will come up for me to put an image URL in.

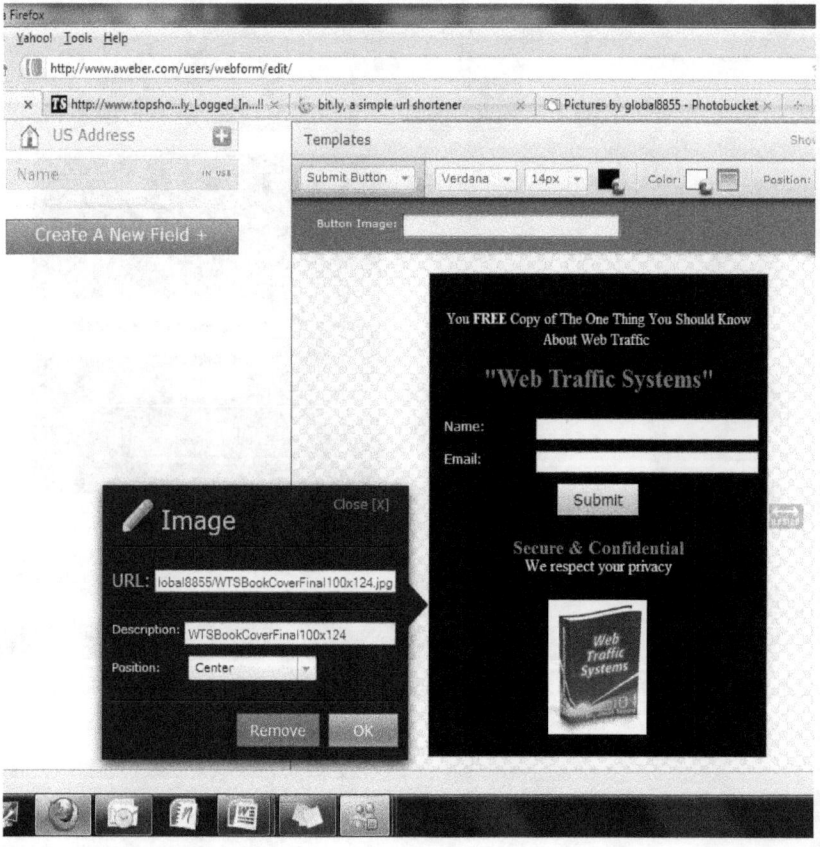

Click ok and then move it up just like you did the first wording

The web form is finished Click go to step 2

Fill in your form name – this will be how you will identify your template on the previous page in "My Templates" and if you make more than one form for this list this will identify which form this is.

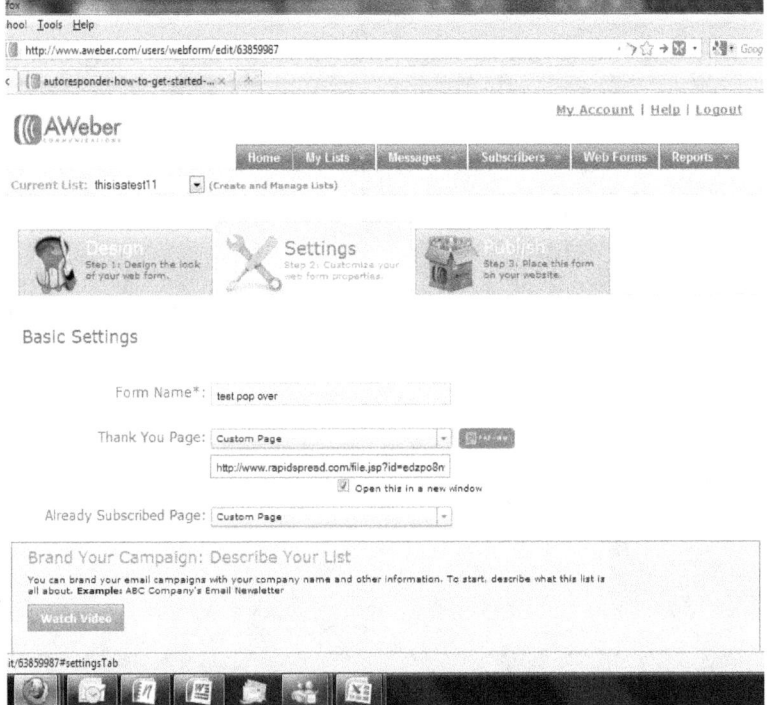

I am using this for as a pop over so I will name this "test pop over" by putting test pop over in where I have it highlighted in blue below

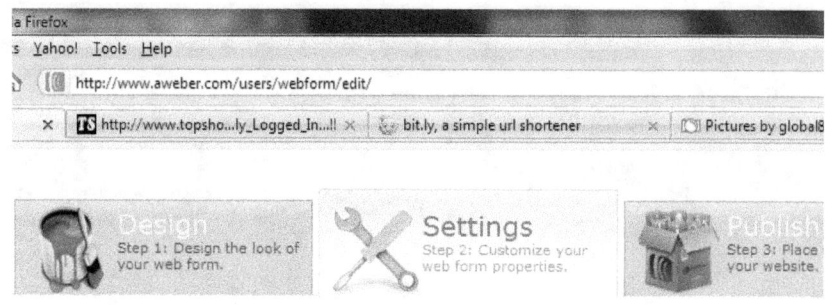

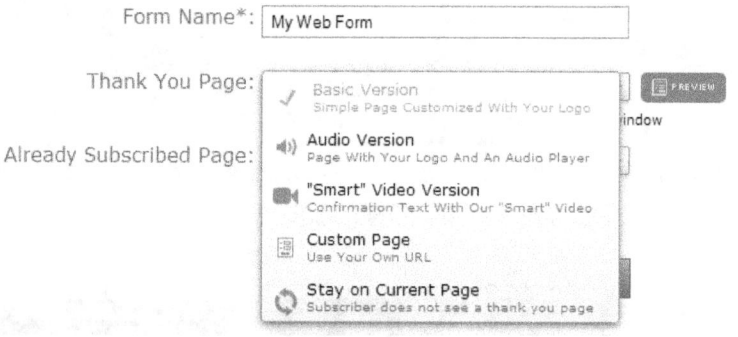

Click the down arrow for the thank you page and choose custom page

Do the same for already subscribed page

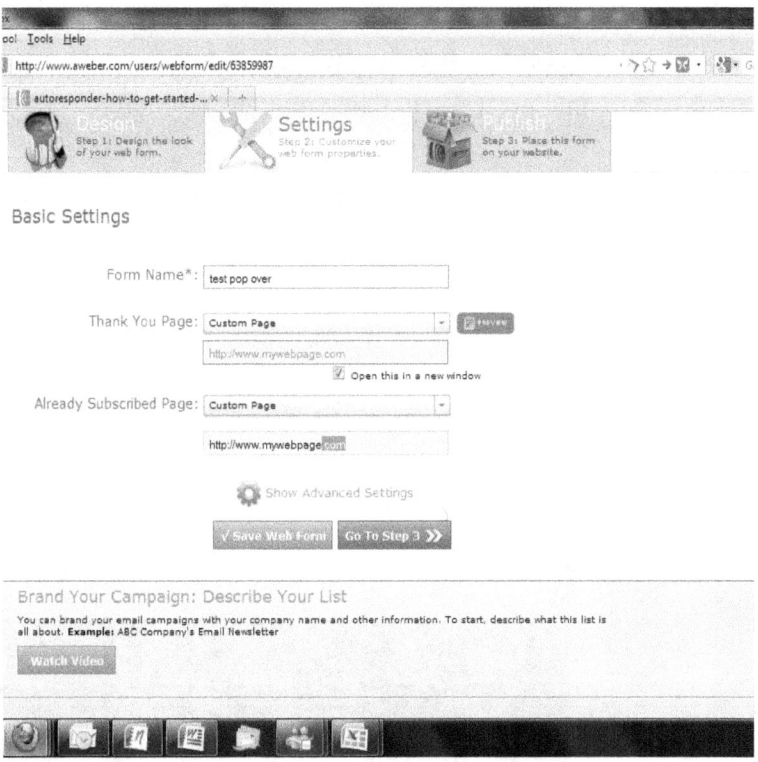

Here I enter the URL for my offer page or the webpage I want the subscriber to visit next. I usually put the same URL in the "Already Subscribed Page"

You can check the open in a new window or not this is a personal preference. Click on "Go To Step 3"

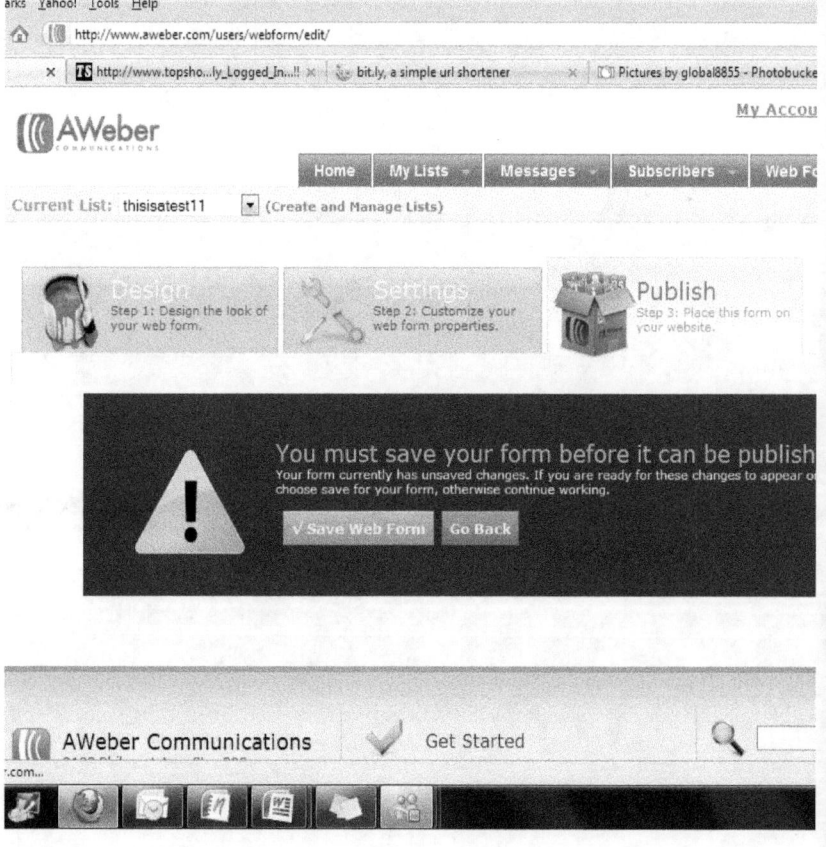

Click save web form in green box

You will now see this page where you can choose how you want to have your form published.

I usually install my own form so I choose the top one.

Below you see the script that is produced to install it yourself.

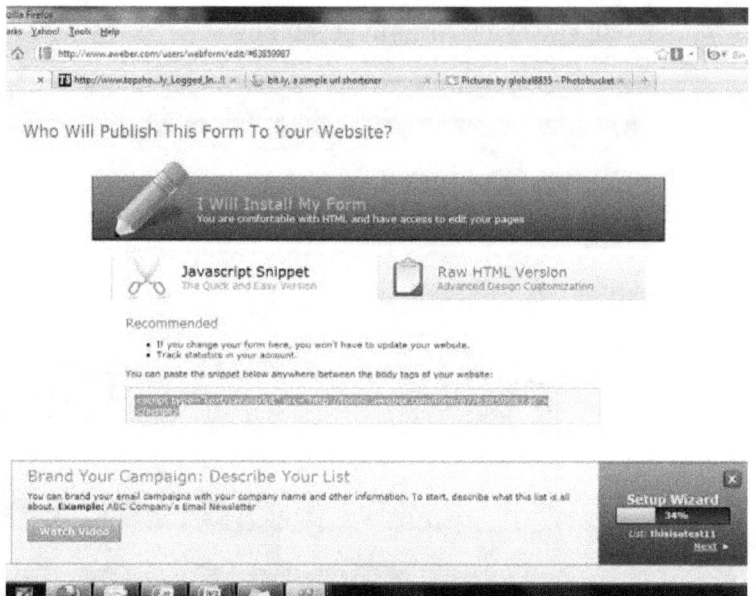

This is the code you would use to install it yourself.

After this code is produced it never changes.

All of the changes that you make on your form or list will automatically be reflected in this code.

So after you install the code you can come back and change anything you want and all changes will be making on your webpage.

There is no need to reinstall the code a second time.

We are now going to go and look at other functions of AWeber in order to communicate with our subscribers.

Go up to the top blue bar and click on "My Lists" and a drop down box will appear.

Choose Confirmed Opt-In.

This will set up what your subscribers will see in the opt-in email that they receive.

This can be as customized as you would like to make it.

Confirmed Opt-In

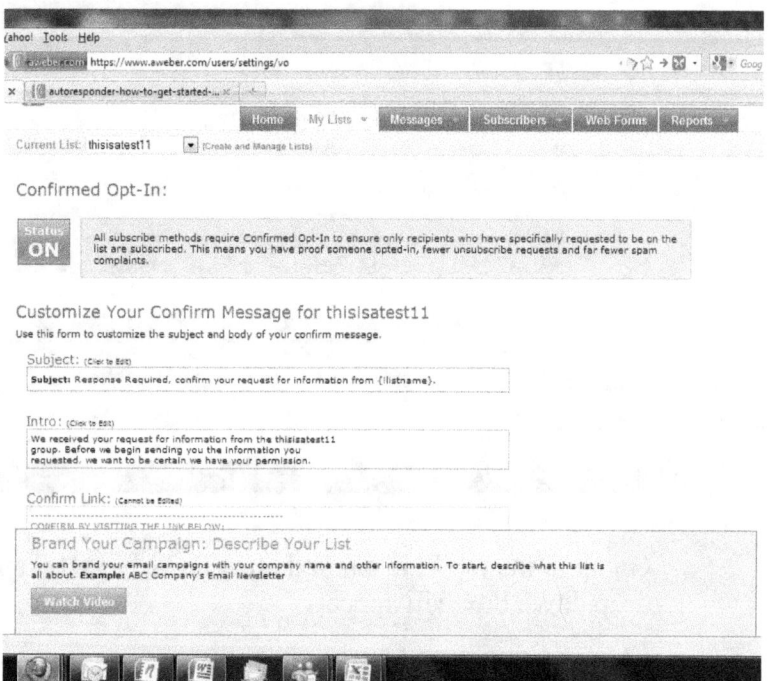

You will see this page.

I will show you how I fill out this page.

There are a lot of choices on this page and it is really a personal preference on a lot of it.

When you click inside the boxes for the different messages the box will open and you can edit the contents.

Subject – I like to use "Confirm your request for information" or "Confirm your Subscription" but there are a lot of other choices also.

Intro – They will have an example of an intro but I usually replace it with one of my own.

If you want the intro to be addressed to the subscriber you can click on the drop down arrow next to the "insert field" and a whole list of possibilities will drop down.

As you can see I have addressed my intro to the subscriber's first name.

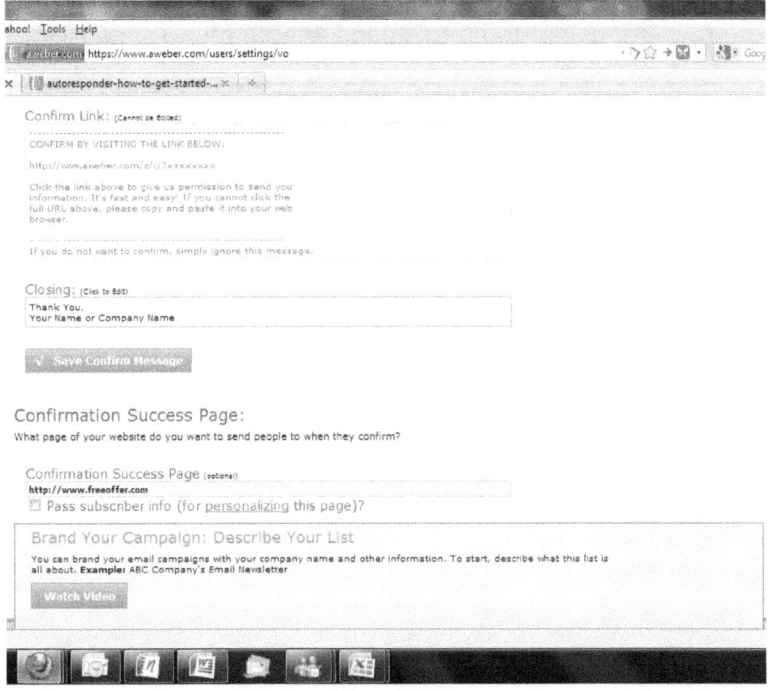

Confirm Link – this cannot be edited.

Closing – I just leave this like they have it. This is where your company name will show up. If you want to edit it, just click on the box.

Confirmation Success Page – This is where Subscribers are sent after they confirm their subscription. Here is where I put the URL for the "Free Offer" I am giving away. The reason I put the URL for the "Free Offer" here and not on the web form is: If they have to confirm in order to get the "Free Offer" then there is more of a chance that the subscriber will confirm. Everyone that confirms I can send follow-up letters to and up-sell other products to them. If I give the subscriber the "Free Offer" as soon as they enter their name and email then they are not as apt to confirm and enable me to send them further offers.

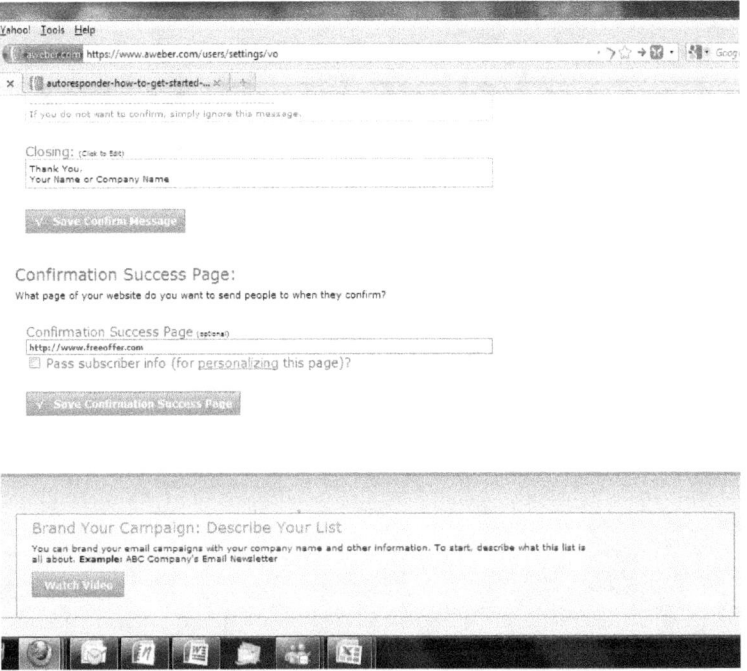

Now click on the green button that says "Save Confirm Message" and on the green button that says "Save confirmation Success Page"

Your confirm opt-in is now finished.

Follow Up Messages

Go to the top bar and click on the blue button "Messages".

When the drop down box comes up click on the "Follow Up" button.

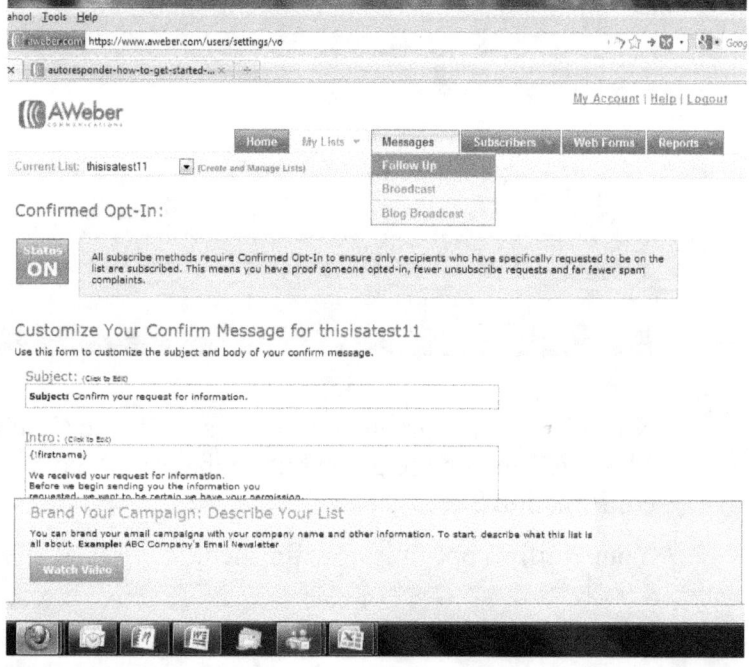

You will see this page

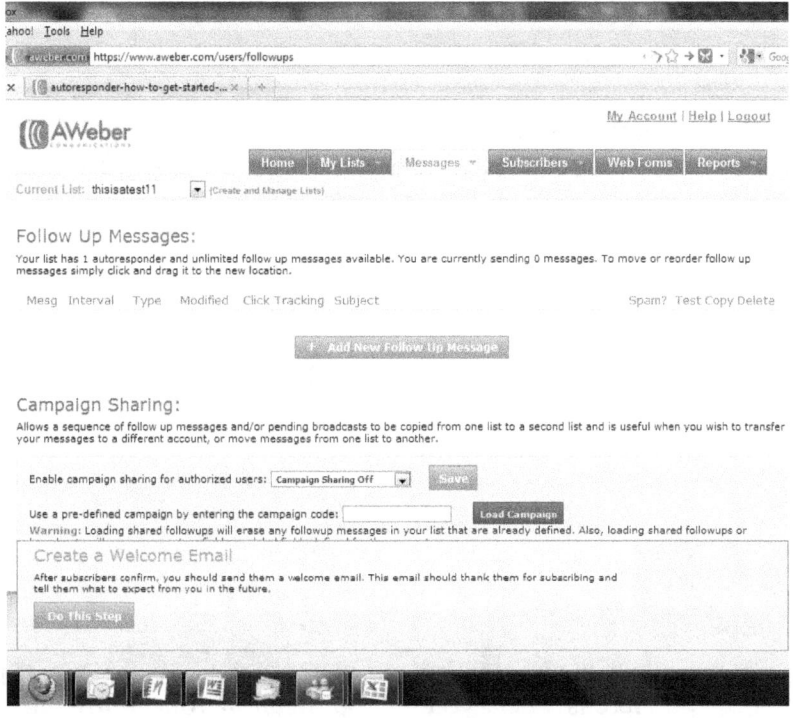

 Click on the green button "+ Add New Follow Up Message"

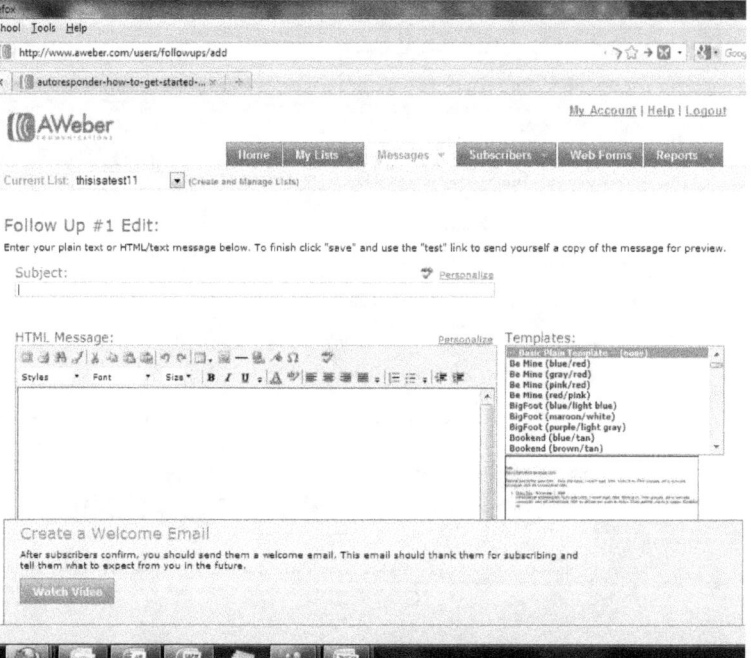

Here is where you will put in all of your follow-up messages.

These will be sales letters.

The first 7 should be selling the product on the web page the person originally went to when they signed up on your list.

After that you can send the subscriber other offers.

So this is basically setting up an e-mail.

Subject – This is but will go in the subject line of the email.

HTML Message – put your message here if it is done in HTML format. I am going to use a text message for this demonstration.

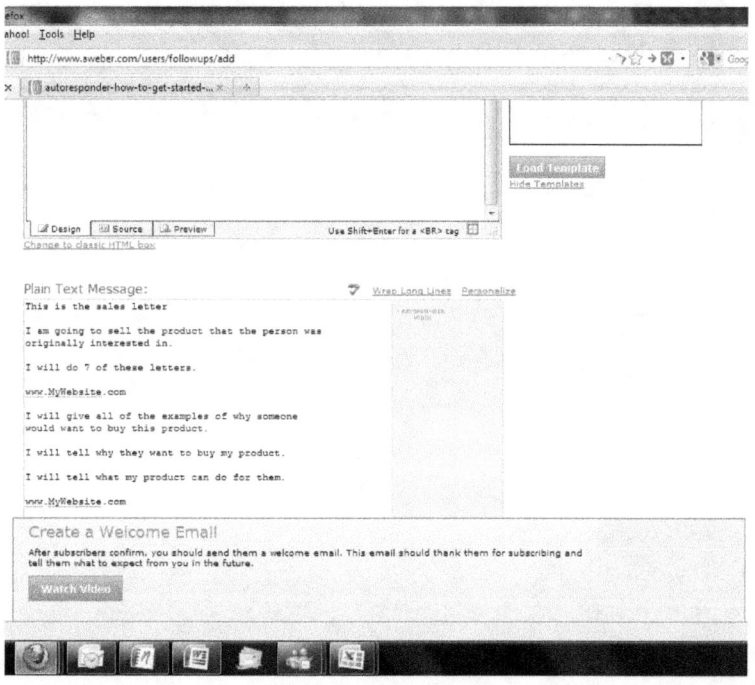

When I scroll down the page I find a box labeled "Plain Text Message"

I will put my sales letter in this spot.

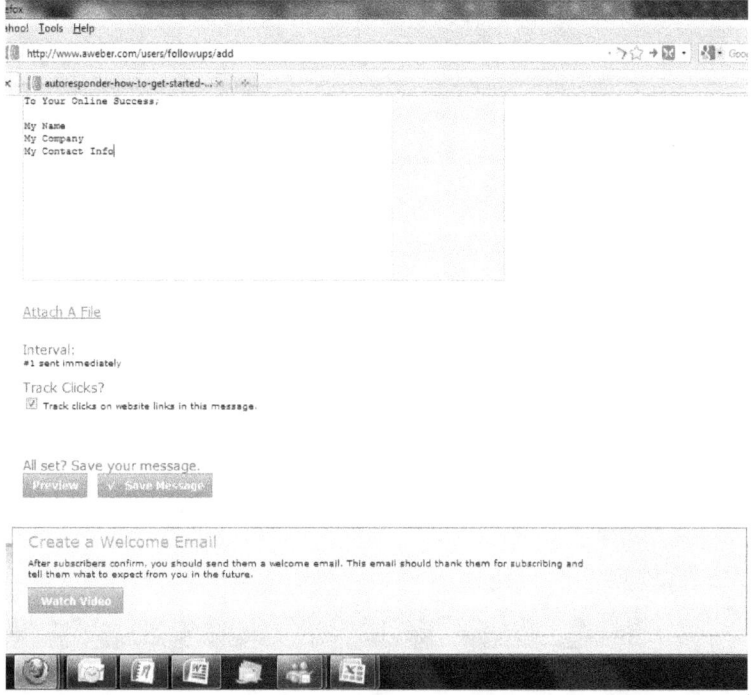

When I scroll down further I find the green button that says "Save Message".

I click on that button and my first sales letter is saved.

This sales letter will be sent out immediately after the subscriber confirms.

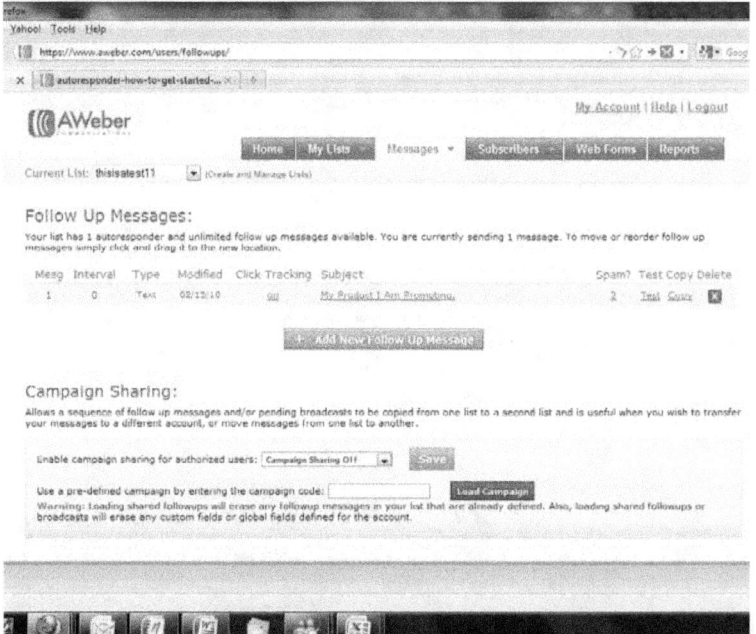

I am sent back to this page.

I see my first sales letter listed.

If you look where it says "Spam?"

There is a 2, any email that has a number less than 5 can be sent. Anything 5 or higher will be considered spam and should not be sent.

Click on the green button "+Add New Follow Up Message" to add your next message.

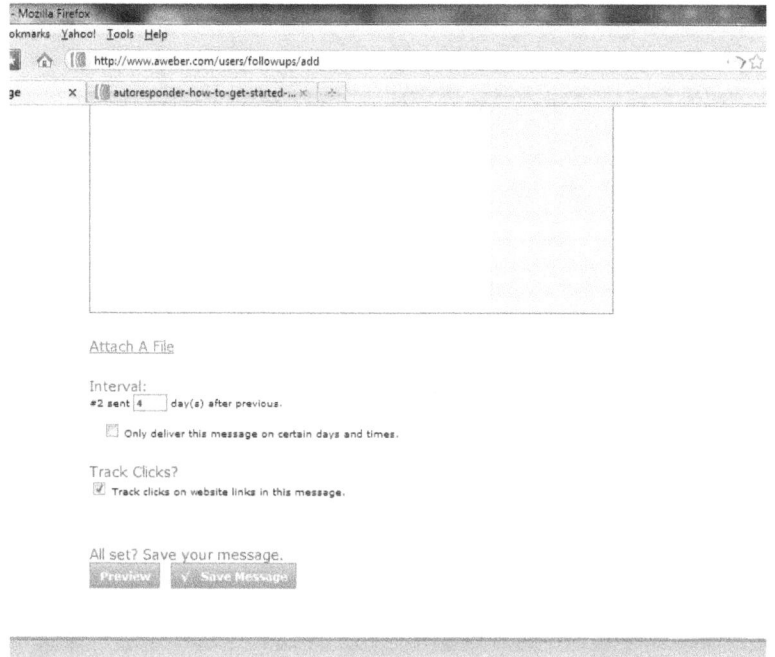

You will repeat the same process for this sales letter.

Notice though that this email will be sent 4 days after the last one.

I usually leave this as they have it but you can change this setting to reflect how often you want an email sent to your subscriber.

Your basic campaign is now set up.

As you grow your list you can go in and add broadcasts of various kinds and can personalize settings to your liking but to start out with you have a campaign that will grow your list and sell your product.

I Have a Special Gift for My Readers

I appreciate my readers for without them I am just another author attempting to make a difference. If my book has made a favorable impression please leave me an honest review. Thank you in advance for you participation.

My readers and I have in common a passion for the written word as well as the desire to learn and grow from books.

My special offer to you is a massive ebook library that I have compiled over the years. It contains hundreds of fiction and non-fiction ebooks in Adobe Acrobat PDF format as well as the Greek classics and old literary classics too.

In fact, this library is so massive to completely download the entire library will require over 5 GBs open on your desktop.

Use the link below and scan all of the ebooks in the library. You can select the ebooks you want individually or download the entire library.

The link below does not expire after a given time period so you are free to return for more books rather than clog your desktop. And feel free to give the link to your friends who enjoy reading too.

I thank you for reading my book and hope if you are pleased that you will leave me an honest review so that I can improve my work and or write books that appeal to your interests.

Okay, here is the link…

http://tinyurl.com/special-readers-promo

PS: If you wish to reach me personally for any reason you may simply write to mailto:support@epubwealth.com.

I answer all of my emails so rest assured I will respond.

Meet the Author

Dr. Leland Benton is Director of Applied Web Info, a holding company for ePubWealth.com, a leading ePublisher company based in Utah. With over 21,000 resellers in over 22-countries, ePubWealth.com is a leader in ePublishing, book promotion, and ebook marketing.

As the creator and author of "The ePubWealth Program," Leland teaches up-and-coming authors the ins-and-outs of today's ePublishing world. He has assisted hundreds of authors make it big in the ePublishing world.

Leland also created a series of external book promotion programs and teaches authors how to promote their books using external marketing sources.

Leland is also the Managing Director of Applied Mind Sciences, the company's mind research unit and Chief Forensics Investigator for the company's ForensicsNation unit. He is active in privacy rights through the company's PrivacyNations unit and is an expert in survival planning and disaster relief through the company's SurvivalNations unit.

Leland resides in Southern Utah.

Visit some of his websites
http://www.AddMeInNow.com
http://www.AppliedMindSciences.com
http://www.BookbuilderPLUS.com
http://www.BookJumping.com
http://www.EmailNations.com
http://www.EmbarrassingProblemsFix.com

http://www.ePubWealth.com
http://www.ForensicsNation.com
http://www.ForensicsNationStore.com
http://www.FreebiesNation.com
http://www.HealthFitnessWellnessNation.com
http://www.Neternatives.com
http://www.PrivacyNations.com
http://www.RetireWithoutMoney.org
http://www.SurvivalNations.com
http://www.TheBentonKitchen.com
http://www.Theolegions.org
http://www.VideoBookbuilder.com

Some Other Books You May Enjoy From ePubWealth.com, LLC Library Catalog

EPW Library Catalog Online
http://www.epubwealth.com/wp-content/uploads/2013/07/Leland-benton-private-turbo.pdf

EPW Library Catalog Download
http://www.filefactory.com/f/562ef3ea1a054f0a

www.ingramcontent.com/pod-product-compliance
Lightning Source LLC
Chambersburg PA
CBHW051821170526
45167CB00005B/2109